*Beautiful Highways*

# THE DOLOMITES

# THE DOLOMITES

80 PHOTOGRAPHS · 8 DRAWINGS · 5 MAPS

THAMES AND HUDSON · LONDON

Translated from the German "Dolomitenland" published by Anton Schroll & Co., Vienna

Photographs by GHEDINA, Cortina d'Ampezzo, except those on pp. 16, 60, 76 (Fritz Benesch, Vienna) and 78 (Foto Ambrosi, Bolzano)

Maps, sketches und jacket designed by Andreas Hemberger, Vienna

Blocks produced by Klischeeanstalt Rasteiger, Graz

Printed in Austria by Christoph Reisser's Söhne, Vienna

American edition published by T. Y. Crowell - Studio Publications New York

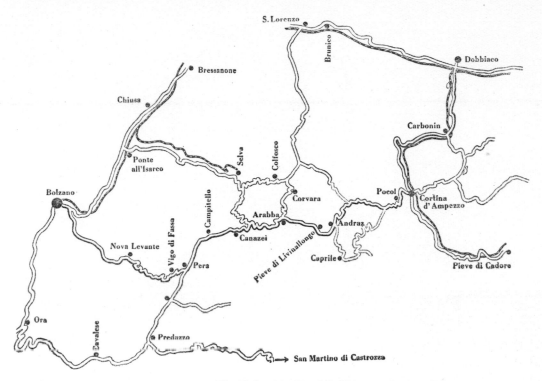

*The Dolomites Road Dobbiaco—Cortina d'Ampezzo—Bolzano*

With the completion in 1909 of the Alpine road connecting Cortina d'Ampezzo with Dobbiaco (Toblach), in what is now the Italian Tyrol, a new and spectacular highway became available to the traveller. It opened up magnificent vistas, enabling those who have neither the time nor the inclination to penetrate the mountain fastnesses of the Dolomites on foot or on ski nevertheless to enjoy a scene of remarkable grandeur.

The Dolomites Road (Strada delle Dolomiti), running from Bolzano to Dobbiaco, and some 87 miles long, follows in part the Strada d'Allemagna which was finished in 1830, to constitute a direct link between northwestern Europe and Venice. In 1860 a road was forged between Bolzano (Bozen) and Nova Levante (Welschnofen), through the Val d'Ega (Eggental), a feat of considerable technical skill. It was the signal for the more intrepid mountaineers to penetrate this hitherto virtually unexplored region, which for centuries had been associated in men's minds with myths and legends. The Catináccio (Rosengarten, so named after the pink glow which often suffuses these mountain peaks at sunrise) was first scaled by the Englishman Tucker in 1874; five years later, Grohmann, an Austrian pioneer of the Dolomites, made the first ascent of the Marmolada, the highest of their summits. Fifteen years after Grohmann's conquest of the "Queen of the Dolomites", the section of the Strada delle Dolomiti between Nova Levante and Vigo di Fassa was finished; then, between 1904 and 1909 the most difficult and complicated portions across the Pordoi and Falzárego passes were engineered.

The Austrians, who were responsible for these projects, saw also the strategic possibilities of such a highway; and, indeed, it was only a few years later that this region became a battle-ground where Austrians and Italians fought during the first World War. Under the Treaty of Saint-Germain (1919) the South Tyrol was ceded to the Italians.

The Dolomites, with their characteristic great limestone buttresses and eroded rocky "fingers" pointing into the skies, are more impressive than many of their appreciably higher neighbours to the West and North; for their impact is more immediate—with the possible exception of the Matterhorn—by virtue of the fact that they rise stark and uncompromising above gentle pastures and wide fertile valleys. When the sun catches their precipitous faces they gleam like marble, which has earned them the epithet "Mountains of Light".

In the ensuing pages the armchair traveller will be taken in comfort along this spectacular highway through the Dolomites, which today, at the height of the season, carries some thousands of mechanically propelled vehicles a day; he will be shown, in a series of breath-taking photographs, not only the most magnificent views but also more homely scenes, such as the farmer tending his sheep, the little church at Corvara deep under snow, and the humble house where the great painter Titian was born. The Notes which accompany the pictures help to place their subjects in geographical, topographical and historical perspective.

*Lago di Dobbiaco*

*The Tre Cime di Lavaredo*

2

3

*The Tre Cime di Lavaredo*

Left: Lago di Landro and
Monte Cristallo (10,550 ft.)

Above: Lago di Misurina (5,758 ft.)
and the Sorapiss mountain group (10,515 ft.)

On Monte Piana: remains of Austrian field defences from the first World War

*Climbing on the
Guglia Edmondo de
Amicis*

7

*On the Passo di Tre Croci (5,935 ft.)*

*The Dolomites Road from Dobbiaco to the Falzárego pass*

1. **The Lago di Dobbiaco** lies at the entrance of the Landro Valley, through which run both the motor road and the Dolomites railway leading to the Valley of Ampezzo. The railway follows the tracks of the old Austrian and Italian military railways and was first opened to the public in 1921.

**2, 3. The Tre Cime di Lavaredo,** towering above the Rienza Gorge, provide the first grand view of high peaks on the Dolomites Road. This is one of the famous Alpine sights and even non-mountaineers will find it worth while to walk up to the tourist hut in order to enjoy the view at closer range.

**4. Lago di Landro and Monte Cristallo.** The lake is shallow and sometimes almost dries up in summer; it is nevertheless a celebrated view in the Dolomites, especially when seen against the dark northern face of Monte Cristallo and the blue reflections from the Cristallo glacier, arcadian beauty and wild grandeur blending superbly.

**5. Lago di Misurina and the Sorapiss mountain group.** The slightly longer route from the Landro Valley to Cortina by way of Lago di Misurina and the Passo di Tre Croci is rewarding for the beauty of its views, the most outstanding of which is Lago di Misurina, whose turquoise waters extend for two thirds of a mile. Mount Sorapiss (10,515 ft.) has glaciers in the gullies leading to the summit. It has a deceptively harmless appearance compared with other peaks in the Dolomites but its ascent should not be attempted by inexperienced climbers.

**6. Austrian field defences on Monte Piana** from the first World War. When the Austrians established their line of defence in the Dolomites War on the mountains overlooking the Landro Valley the summit of Mount Piana, because of its dominating position, was the scene of much heavy fighting. The northern slope was held by the Austrians, the southern one by the Italians. Like the Col di Lana, this mountain became one of the blood-bathed peaks of the Dolomites. The summit can easily be reached from Misurina by the military road (3 m.). Like on other battlefields in the Dolomites, a shadow is cast over the view by ghosts from the past.

**7. Guglia Edmondo de Amicis,** above Lago di Misurina, is an isolated needle of rock standing straight and slender. It was first climbed in 1906 by the following device: a rope was thrown round its top, bridging the intervening chasm and the climbers crossed over hanging from the rope by their hands.

**8. On the Passo di Tre Croci**—The three crosses from which the pass derives its name are said to have been erected in memory of a mother and her two children, who froze to death at this point in 1709.

**9—13. Cortina d'Ampezzo** lies in a broad part of the valley surrounded by precipitous peaks (among them Cristallo, Sorapiss und Tofano each have a height of over 10,000 feet). It is the starting point for climbs of other famous peaks, such as the Tre Cime di Lavaredo, Antelao, Pelmo, etc. The first record of Cortina dates back to A. D. 1000. When climbing in the Dolomites became popular this village soon acquired fame as a tourist centre and fashionable summer and winter resort. The local people were quick to recognize the possibilities of skiing and received winter sport addicts as early as the turn of the century. Their enthusiasm will be rewarded by the holding in Cortina of the Winter Olympic Games of 1956. Many rope railways and ski lifts carry visitors to the heights around Cortina. The most famous is the Faloria rope railway which has a length of $1^1/_2$ miles and rises 2873 feet, gliding over gorges and peaks and affording a superb view into the very heart of the Dolomites.

*Cortina d'Ampezzo
with the ski-slopes of
the Col Drusciè and
the Tofana*

10

*Over the valley and
above the clouds —
the Faloria rope
railway*

**13**    *Left: Winter's pleasures in the skiers' paradise on Mount Faloria (6,975 ft.)*          *Above: Winter's beauty. On Mount Faloria*

14

*Left: Springtime in the Dolomites*

*Above: Not far from Cortina lies the picturesque village of Pieve di Cadore. In the small farm-house with the marble memorial tablet Titian was born*

*The road to the*
*Passo di*
*Falzárego and the*
*Tofana di Rozes*
*(4,620 ft.)*

14. **Springtime in the Dolomites**

15. **The house where Titian was born in Pieve di Cadore.** On the road which links Cortina with Venice, by way of Belluno, there still stands the small farmhouse where, in 1477, Titian was born. The painter who raised the art of painting in Venice to new heights owned large tracts of forests and valleys in the Dolomites and traded profitably in timber, thus showing that a great painter can also be a good businessman.

16, 20, 21. **The road over the Passo di Falzárego.** From Cortina the road climbs to the pass with looped bends from which one enjoys lovely views. It has an average gradient of rather less than 1 in 12 and rises 2942 feet up to the Passo di Falzárego. The descent to Pieve di Livinallongo has a gradient of 1 in 12, much of it over very rough and difficult ground, where the road has been built on concrete retaining walls or hewn out of the rock. This stretch contains one of the most interesting engineering feats of the Dolomites Road, the Falzárego Tunnel. It is built on a curve throughout the whole 181 feet of its length.

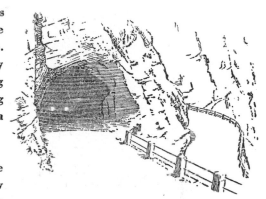

17. **The South face of the Tofana di Rozes**

18, 19. **The Cinque Torri.** The five bizarre towers of rock which dominate the Passo di Falzárego are Cortina's own climbing ground. The mighty crags grow abruptly out of rich green fields. Torre Grande has a height of 525 feet, 160 feet higher than the cross on the dome of St. Paul's. At the foot of the Cinque Torri, even non-mountaineers have the chance to see rock climbing at close range.

22. **The Marmolada** from the Passo di Falzárego

23. **The ruins of Andraz Castle at the foot of Col di Lana.** The castle was built in the 12th century as the seat of the High Order of Brixen. One must try to picture it without the road in order to get an idea of the wild mountain scene which this castle once dominated. The fact that it stands close to the mountain which became a point of great strategic importance and the scene of much fighting in the first World War, suggests that the value of this site had been recognised even in the Middle Ages.

24. **Monument to the dead of the Col di Lana**

25. **Clouds form a cross over the Col di Lana.** This picture is famous—it can be found in almost every family album in the region of the Dolomites, regardless of which side the father had been fighting on. It was on a day in no way out of the ordinary that this black cloud-cross appeared over the Col di Lana and it was pure chance that a photographer roaming around in the mountains happened to be ready with his camera at that precise moment. Yet this photograph, taken by pure chance, carried with it a message which moved the hearts of men for many a year.

26. **Pieve di Livinallongo** was completely destroyed during the first World War. The new Pieve again fits effortlessly into the landscape and bears witness to the good taste of its inhabitants. The immense rock face in the background, whose breadth is $2/3$ of a mile—the most mighty "wall" in the Dolomites—is the north-western face of the Civetta, the "Queen of all Walls", as the Italians call it. Its height is 3608 feet.

*Routes up the south face of the Tofana di Rozes:* **▬** *Dimai route;* **- - -** *Stoesser route;* **. . . .** *Tissi route*

*THE SOUTHERN FACE OF THE TOFANA DI ROZES. The road to the Falzárego Pass winds to the summit along the base of the majestic southern face of the Tofana di Rozes. It is an unforgettable sight and anyone who has seen it must wonder whether such a wall can be scaled. There are many climbing routes, of varying difficulty. The degree of difficulty is classified in a scale which goes from 1 to 6. Dimaï's "classical" route was opened in 1901 by the professional guides Dimai, Siorpaes and Verzi with two young ladies, the baronesses Ilona and Rolanda von Eötvös. Even today this is considered a very difficult test of rock-climbing ability and experienced climbers employ six hours to reach the summit by the Dimai route. The ideal routes lead straight to the summit through the orange-coloured shaft; these are the Tissi and Stoesser routes, but they are both extremely difficult (sixth degree of difficulty).*

*The South side of the Tofana di Rozes above the road to the Passo di Falzárego*

*Climbing on the Torre
Grande of the Cinque
Torri*

18

*The Torre Grande*
*of the Cinque Torri*

*Left: The road to the Passo di Falzárego with
the Sasso di Stria — the "Witches' Stone"*

*Below: The road to the Passo di Falzárego
(6,903 ft.) and the Cortina mountains*

*At the top of the Passo di Falzárego La Marmolada (10, 965 ft.) comes into view.*
*The gleam of its silver-white summit is visible for long stretches of the Dolomites Road*

*Andraz Castle*

23

*Monument to the dead of the Col di Lana on the road to the Passo di Falzárego*

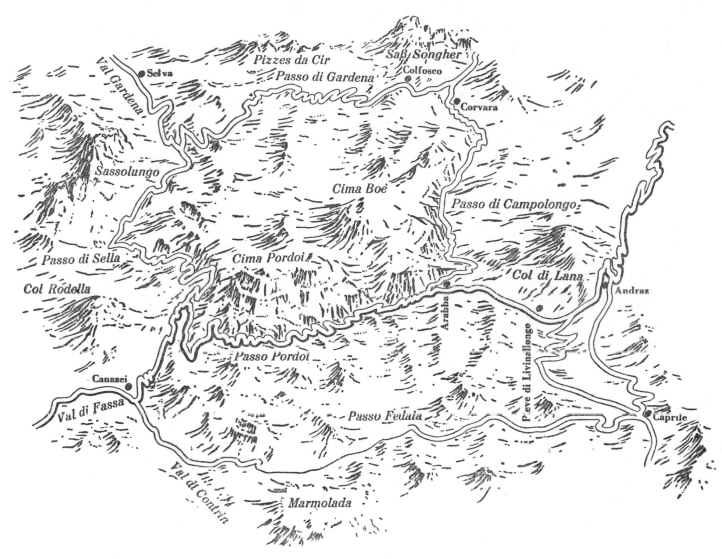

The Dolomites Road from the Falzárego pass to Canazei

How the Dolomites front advanced
during the first World War

THE WAR ON THE COL DI LANA. *Looking down from the top of the Piz Boé, the peak with the most famous view in the Dolomites, one readily understands why the Col di Lana acquired such strategic importance in this theatre during the first World War, in spite of its rather inconspicuous appearance when viewed from the valley. As long as the Austrians could hold on to the Col di Lana they could control a deep area behind the Italian front. Until the Italians managed to capture it they were unable to move or set up an alternative front in this sector. For both sides, the Col di Lana became "Col di Sangue"—Mountain of Blood. After months of violent but unsuccessful attacks, in December 1915 the Italian High Command decided to adopt the plan of Lieutenant Caetani, an engineer, to blow up the summit of the mountain with its defenders. Early in January, Austrian observers at the Passo Pordoi reported large heaps of debris growing under the summit of the Col di Lana, but it was believed that there was nothing more to it than the building of new underground positions. By the middle of March, however, there was no longer any doubt that the Italians were mining the mountain. Suggestions by the front-line officers to withdraw from the Col di Lana and recapture it after the mine had been exploded were refused by the Austrian Supreme Command, which limited itself to ordering counter-tunnelling. But it was too late for that. The Italian artillery increased their fire on all accesses to the summit and by April 12 their tunnelling was completed. On the night of April 15, five tons of high explosive were placed in the explosion chamber. The Austrian garrison on the summit was now under a ghastly strain: the noise of the drills — irritating as they might have been — had stopped and the silence only meant that at any minute the mountain would blow up. On April 15 a non-stop artillery barrage descended on the Austrian strongpoints, systematically flattening them out. 140 guns of all calibres were directed at the Col di Lana. In the evening of April 17, the last Austrian signal from the Col di Lana was received: "Situation desperate —please send immediate help". At 11.30 that night the mine was exploded by electric detonators. With a deafening noise the mountain split open. 10,000 tons of rock heaved up and away. The artillery barrage was increased and Italian infantry started to attack. 170 defenders posted below the summit had survived but were stunned by the explosion and taken prisoner. Only one man survived out of the detachment of 200 Kaiserjäger, the mountain troops, stationed on the summit. All the others had been buried in the enormous crater.*

*Clouds form a cross above the Col di Lana*

25

*Pieve di Livinal-longo and the Civetta (10,558 ft.)*

26

*Arabba and the
Col di Lana
(8,084 ft.)*

*The road over the Campolongo Saddle (6,151 ft.), the Lago Boé*
*and — with their cloud-capped peaks — the Pelmo (centre) and*
*the Civetta (right), both over 10,000 ft. high*

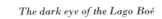
*The dark eye of the Lago Boé*

*The Sass Songher*
*(8,743 ft.)*

*The charming church at Colfosco, the Sella group and the Val de Mesdi (left) with the Dent de Mesdi*

**27. Arabba.** This is the last village before the road twists its way in innumerable bends up to the Passo Pordoi. Arabba is also the starting point for the route round the mighty massif of peaks of the Sella group, across the Campolongo saddle. It takes in the passes of Gardena and Sella, which offer even more grandiose views than does the road over the Passo Pordoi.

**28, 29. The Campolongo Saddle and Lake Boé.** It is one hour's walk from the green meadows of the Campolongo saddle into the grey, rocky wilderness of the Sella group. Although it is surrounded by roads, the Sella group, a rock-massif of nearly 8 square miles, is one of the most virgin and unspoiled areas in the Dolomites. According to an old Ladin legend told locally, the small lake is the home of a dangerous dragon who comes out at night and flies over the land spitting fire.

**30, 31. Corvara and the Sass Songher.** Corvara Ladinia, as it is also called, is the centre of the Ladin-speaking area. It is a small community with a lovely 15th-century church, surrounded by green sloping meadows, with the picturesque Sass Songher towering in the background. With its wide fields and its fascinating mountains Corvara rightly enjoys the fame of a pleasant resort for winter sports.

**32, 33. Colfosco and the Val de Mesdi.** From Colfosco on the road to the Passo Gardena the Val de Mesdi leads up to the Sella plateau... "a wild, fabulous, terrifying circus from which not a glimpse of the world of the living is possible, where everything is dead, silent, wild, steep and dangerous, provoking both fear and admiration."—such was the impression made by the dark Val de Mesdi and its sky-high precipices on a traveller only a few decades ago. A walk of five hours through the Val de Mesdi leads to the Piz Boé (10,339 ft.), the highest point of the Sella plateau, surrounded by steep slopes on all sides. The show piece of the Val de Mesdi is a rocky needle, the Dent de Mesdi, which takes on a peculiar shape also when viewed from the road.

*THE LADINS. The Ladin people are to be found right across the Dolomite area (around the Dolomites Road from Cortina to the Passo di Costalunga). The Ladins would seem to be the Latinised descendants of the Rhaetic peoples who originated from Veneto-Illyrian, Celtic and Etruscan tribes. Little is known of the Etruscans, but it has been established that they inhabited the Alpine area about 500 B.C. At the beginning of the Christian Era these local tribes were subsequently driven by the Romans right into the higher valleys of the Alps where, although they lost their political independence, they were still able to preserve their national character up to our times. The most peculiar aspect of the Ladins is undoubtedly their language, which consists of expressions from pre-historic ages, Etruscan word roots and Latin words. This living relic of ancient times has been preserved in the seclusion of the mountains right into the age of the atom.*

**34—36.** The road to the Passo di Gardena was built by the Austrians during the first World War for military use and it was planned so as not to afford too easy a target for artillery rather than for its views and as a way of approach to beauty spots. Formerly the pass was reached by a rough and narrow track. The pass itself lies in a truly alpine landscape and the road passes through a defile with towering walls of rock on either side.

**37.** The Chair lift to the Passo di Gardena. This chair lift follows the Val Antercepis over the old path known as far back as the 14th century. The climb up to the Passo Gardena used to be strenuous but now it has become a pleasant ride, vaguely reminiscent of the faster joys of a roundabout.

**38.** The ruined Castello di Valle in the Val Gardena. The castle was built in the early middle ages against the rocky face of the Stelvio which is 1476 feet high. By the 16th century it had already begun to fall into dilapidation. It is the birthplace of the minstrel Oswald von Wolkenstein (1367) who ran away from home at the age of ten. Much later, when he had become a famous poet who was honoured by queens, he sang:

> "Three pennies in my pocket
> and a crust of bread
> was all I carried
> when I ran into need."

In his old age, after a very full life, he returned to the quiet valley of Gardena.

**39.** Castel Gardena (Fischburg Castle) near St. Christina. Built 1622—41 by Engelhard Dietrich von Wolkenstein, this castle looks more inviting than the dark stronghold of Wolkenstein, but is still buttressed with martial towers. It is one of the last of its kind, later palaces being progressively adapted to more expansive times of peace.

**40, 41.** In the Val Gardena. The valley culminates and ends with the most impressive of all its views—the Sasso Lungo, a bastion almost 2 miles long, and over 10,000 feet high. Together with Pelmo and Civetta, it is the most impressive crest of the Dolomites. The Val Gardena, however, enjoys an almost southern climate, with vines growing on its lower slopes. St. Christina and Ortisei are the largest villages of the valley and both are starting points for walks to the Alpe di Siusi, a wide plateau, a perfect garden of wild flowers in summer and an ideal skiing ground in winter. The "Vogelweidhof" in Lajen-Ried is held to be the birthplace of Walther von der Vogelweide. Two celebrated Minnesingers were born in the Val Gardena. Val Gardena woodcarvers are well known. Their art was recognised early in the 18th century and has evoked ever wider response. Their expressive icons and crucifixes can be seen on many roadsides.

*View from the Sella plateau to the Val de Mesdi; to the left, the Dent de Mesdi,*
*with, far below, the road to the Passo di Gardena*

Right : On the Passo
di Gardena

Left: The road to the
Passo di Gardena

*The Passo di
Gardena and the
Pizzes da Cir
(8,520 ft.)*

36

*Across hills and gorges: the chair-lift to the Passo di Gardena*

*The ruined
Castello di Valle in the
Val Gardena*

*Two bastions: Castel
Gardena (seat of the
Counts of
Wolkenstein) near
St. Cristina,
dominated by the
Sasso Lungo*

39

*Above the alpine pastures of the Val Gardena: the Sasso Lungo (10,426 ft.)*

*Right: wooden carved crucifix in the Val Gardena*

**40**

*Alpine hotel where
the roads to the
Passo di Gardena
and to the Passo
di Sella meet*

**43** *The Passo di Sella (7,277 ft.) and the gigantic limestone plateau of the Sella*

*The Passo di Sella and the Torri di Sella*

*The Sasso Lungo group seen from the Passo di Sella*

*The Col Rodella (8,156 ft.) — one of the most famous viewpoints of the Dolomites*      *Right: The Col Rodella in Winter*      **46**

*Outposts of vegetation*

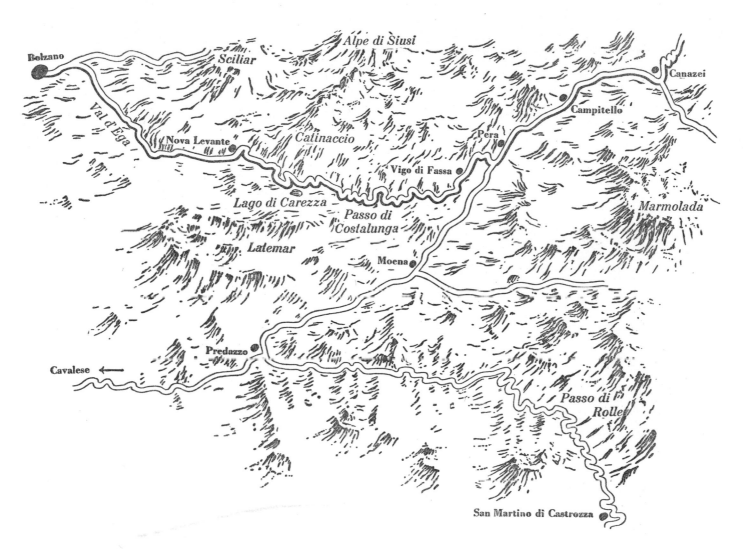

The Dolomites Road from Canazei to Bolzano

**42—45, 50—53. On the road to the Passo di Sella.** By following the road up to the Passo di Sella, which was also built during the first World War, the tour round the Sella group is completed. On this pass the peculiar charm of the Dolomites is seen at its best in the striking contrast between rough, bare rock and the gentle, green meadows. The Passo di Sella is wedged between the steep rock faces of two groups, the Sella and the Sasso Lungo. In the Alps it is easy to lose one's sense of proportion: seen from the pass the Sasso Lungo looks like a big toy of stone and one hardly appreciates that its height from the road varies between 1600 and 3300 feet. The main peak in this group is the Sasso Lungo proper. Long after the Matterhorn had been conquered nobody had yet attempted to climb the Sasso Lungo. The first ascent was made in 1869 by Paul Grohmann with the guides P. Salcher and F. Innerkofler, who were the pioneers of climbing in the Dolomites. Next to the Sasso Lungo, the Punta delle Cinque Dita is dwarfed. Nevertheless, it was always traditionally described as the most difficult mountain in the Alps and the first ascent by Robert Hans Schmitt of Vienna in 1890 did not destroy its reputation.

**46, 47. Col Rodella**

**48. Outposts of vegetation**

**49. Flocks of sheep in the mountains**

**54, 55. The road to the Passo Pordoi.** Winding backwards and forwards through a succession of over 60 hairpin bends, the road from Arabba to Canazei rises 2066 feet and then drops 2558 feet in a distance of just under 14 miles. The average gradient is 1 in 12. "The effortless grace and ease with which this road progresses over rough country" were praised when this route was opened and are outstanding even today. The Passo Pordoi is the highest point of the Dolomites Road. Climbing the Sasso di Pordoi from the pass presents no special difficulty but is strenuous. The road crosses a large moraine (visible at the right of the photograph).

**56, 57. The Passo Pordoi and the Marmolada seen from the way up to the Sasso di Pordoi.** The Passo Pordoi is the starting point of one of the most beautiful Alpine paths: a three hours' walk along the "Vial del Pan" takes one to the Passo Fedaia, which is the gateway to the ice world of the Marmolada glacier.

**58, 59. The Marmolada** is the highest mountain of the Dolomites, with an extensive glacier on its northern slopes. The summit can be reached with comparative ease by way of the glacier. But it was first climbed only in 1864 after numerous unsuccessful attempts. A small hut has been built near the summit where climbers can quench their thirst with hot tea or iced drinks, according to season. During the first World War the front line crossed the Marmolada glacier. Many miles of tunnels were dug in the ice, making the glacier into a gigantic molehill. Nowadays, the only clashes on the glacier are friendly ones: ski races are held on the Marmolada, which is considered the fastest course in the world.

**60. The Sasso Lungo group from the Val di Contrin**

*Close to the motor road the shepherd still tends his flock*

*Left : Hairpin bend on the road to the Passo di Sella.*
*Far beyond is the West face of the Cima di Pordoi*

*Above : The road to the Passo di Sella, looking towards the Marmolada*

*The last spurs of the Sella group: the Piz Ciavazzes and, to the left of them, a distant view of the Torri di Sella*   **52**

*The linked curves of the road to the Passo di Pordoi, looking towards Arabba*

*Passo di Pordoi (7,348 ft.) and Cima di Pordoi (9,685 ft.)*

55

*View on the way up to the Cima di Pordoi: the Passo di Pordoi with the Marmolada*

*The Marmolada and its glacier*

*Right: Ice-bridge on the Marmolada glacier*

*The Sasso Lungo group seen from the Val di Contrin near Canazei*

*Fontanazzo
in the Val
di Fassa*

61

*Pera in the Val di Fassa with the crags and towers of the Catináccio ( Rosengarten )*

In the green Val
di Fassa

*The Torre di
Vaiolet in the
Catináccio
(Rosengarten)*

64

**61—63. In the Val di Fassa.** At Canazei the Dolomites Road reaches the Val di Fassa, which is the name of the upper course of the River Avisio. After the high peaks of the Passo Pordoi or the Passo di Sella, this wide, green valley, dotted with picturesque villages, has an air of gentleness. According to legend, this peaceful valley was once terrorised by mysterious cavemen, the "Bregostans", who were supposed to have been savages, who hunted for their food and robbed their peaceful neighbours. Their descendants were said to have been still living in the nearby forests until a few centuries ago. Perhaps it was due to the legendary Bregostans that the ancient inhabitants of the Val di Fassa showed a great sense of social solidarity and the area federated under a provincial council which could even boast a small mercenary army, the "Arimans". When the Arimans lit their danger beacons to warn the valley below, it was mostly against the approach of marauders bearing the arms of the Counts of Wolkenstein from the Val Gardena.

**64, 65. In the Catináccio (Rosengarten).** The three rocky towers known as the Torri di Vaiolet are probably the most bizarre of all the fantastic peaks in which the Dolomites abound and for many years they have been a powerful magnet for travellers in these parts. There is a chair lift from Vigo di Fassa to Ciampedíe, and this brings the base of the Torri di Vaiolet within easy reach of everyone. A wide path leads from the chair lift station through the Vaiolet valley to the heart of the Catináccio. The three Vaiolet towers have been named after the men who first climbed them: Delago tower (climbed 1895), Stabeler tower (1892), Winkler tower (1887). The central tower (Stabeler) is comparatively easy to climb; at the height of the summer the small terrace at the top is hardly big enough to harbour all the climbers.

*THE LEGEND OF KING LAURIN'S GARDEN OF ROSES. Where the sky now looks down on bare rocks and dizzy precipices there was once the kingdom of Laurin, king of the dwarfs — a magnificent garden of roses in bloom which led to the entrance of the castle inside a hollow mountain. The castle was guarded by 20,000 dwarfs and five giants. The king of the dwarfs kidnapped Similda, sister of Dietlieb of Styria, and brought her to his castle. Dietlieb sought help from his friend Dietrich of Bern and together they set out with their armed followers to free the beautiful Similda. They climbed up to the garden and trampled the dwarf king's beloved roses underfoot. King Laurin went out to meet them wearing a belt that gave him the strength of 12 men and a cap that made him invisible. But during the fight Dietrich tore off the belt and Laurin had to surrender. Thereupon they went into the castle and King Laurin entertained the knights until they were dead drunk. He then had them chained and thrown into the dungeons. But Dietrich melted the chains with his fiery breath and the battle with the dwarfs and the five giants began afresh. And this time the king of the dwarfs was utterly and finally defeated. The knights took him to Bern as a jester for their entertainment. But the captured dwarf longed for his garden of roses and took to flight. From that day no one has ever again seen King Laurin's Garden of Roses — he cursed it and changed it into stone. But towards evening when the setting sun shines on the rocky faces and peaks and they glow as if on fire, then little imagination is needed to recognise the Garden of Roses of the old legend.*

**66, 67. Over the Passo di Rolle to San Martino di Castrozza.** At Vigo di Fassa the road to Predazzo branches off the Dolomites Road. From Predazzo one can take the road over the Passo di Rolle to the internationally famous mountain resort of San Martino di Castrozza. San Martino, surrounded by green fields and woods, lies at the foot of the beautiful group of peaks known as the Pala di San Martino. The village consists almost entirely of hotels and when the season is over and the shutters up it has only about 300 inhabitants. San Martino and the Passo di Rolle are dominated by the Cimone della Pala, the "Matterhorn" of the Dolomites.

**69—71. Over the Passo di Costalunga** the Dolomites Road leads to one of its great beauty spots, the Lago di Carezza. At the end of the last century, the pass was crossed only by a very rough path. The Lago di Carezza is surrounded by forests of dark fir trees and its emerald green waters mirror the milk-white peaks and crags of the Latemar group. The huge Lago di Carezza Hotel near the lake is like a small town, with its 235 rooms, golf course, tennis-courts, shops, workshops and post office. It is a survival of the grand era before the first World War when hotels were built in the style of palaces in which people "resided".

**72. Nova Levante on the Dolomites Road**

**73. The Alpe di Siusi and the Sciliar.** Between the Val Gardena and the Dolomites Road in the Val d'Ega lies a stretch of mountain landscape which can be considered typical of the South Tyrol. The Alpe di Siusi is a green, smooth plateau about forty miles round, at an average height of 6500 feet. It is an ideal holiday resort in either summer or winter with plenty of comfortable hotels. The Sciliar towers above the Alpe di Siusi; its rocky profile forms a characteristic buttress of the Dolomites as seen from the West.

**74—76. In the Val d'Ega.** Not far from Bolzano one encounters perhaps the most romantic stretch in the whole length of the Dolomites Road—the gorge of the Val d'Ega which is so narrow that the road had to be carved into the rock for many a mile. At times it forms a corridor between precipitous smooth walls of porphyry, at others it dives into tunnels or crosses the foaming Ega river over dizzy bridges. Shortly before the valley opens up again one catches sight of the picturesque Castle of Carnedo. It was built during the 13th century and later became the property of the house of Lichtenstein. When the Lichtensteiners and other barons staged a revolt against their ruler, Duke Frederick "of the empty pocket", the latter reduced the castle in spite of its strong fortifications and the steep rock cliffs.

*THE DOLOMITES. In 1789, Deodat de Dolomieu, a Knight of the Maltese Order and an amateur scientist, found a mineral in the Alps with the appearance of chalk, but on which acids made little impression. French scientists called this mineral (whose chemical composition was calcium and magnesium carbonate) "Dolomie" to honour its discoverer. The mountains, south of the Val Pusteria, where this mineral was mainly found, were called the Dolomite mountains, or Dolomites. It was the time when mountaineers first began to climb the peaks, and throughout the world the word "Dolomites" soon became synonymous with wonderland.*

*In the Val di Vaiolet*

*The road over the Passo di Rolle (6,510 ft.)*     *Right: The Cimone della Pala (10,450 ft.) seen from the Passo di Rolle. The column reminds us that battles were fought during the first World War even beneath this majestic mountain*

*San Martino di Castrozza and the Rosetta (8,996 ft.)*

*On the Passo di
Costalunga
(5,752 ft.)*

*Left: Hotel at the Lago di Carezza*

*Right: The Lago di Carezza amid the fir-woods, and the Latemar group*

*Left: Nova Levante*     72

*The flower-carpeted plateau of the Alpe di Siusi and the rocky slope of the Sciliar*

*Two views of the*
*Val d'Ega*

77    *Left: Castello Cornedo in the Val d'Ega*                    *Above: In the Valle Isarco near Bolzano*

*A charming view of Bolzano*

*Bolzano and La Mendola*

*The Catináccio (Rosengarten) seen from Bolzano*

*Runkelstein Castle near Bolzano*

**77. In the Valle Isarco near Bolzano**

**78, 79. Bolzano.** Those breaths from the South, which the Northern traveller may have sensed even in Innsbruck, are strong and fully in evidence by the time he reaches Bolzano. The contrast between North and South is very apparent; glistening snowfields, snowy crests and rugged peaks form a provocative backcloth for the vineyards and orchards, the fig-trees, chestnut trees, cypresses and laurels growing in the valleys near the town. "Trees and plants subsisting precariously at greater heights, here are full of strength and vitality; the sun shines hotly and once again one can believe in God", Goethe wrote in his *Travels to Italy*.

Bolzano is situated in a small plain surrounded by mountains. The town stands near the confluence of three rivers (the Talvera flows into the Isarco and the Isarco into the Adige). It is the junction of important arterial roads. From time immemorial, the lifeline between North and South, over the Brenner Pass, has gone via Bolzano. Through the ages the town increasingly developed into a trading centre and to this day, trade is the main source of its wealth. The style of the town

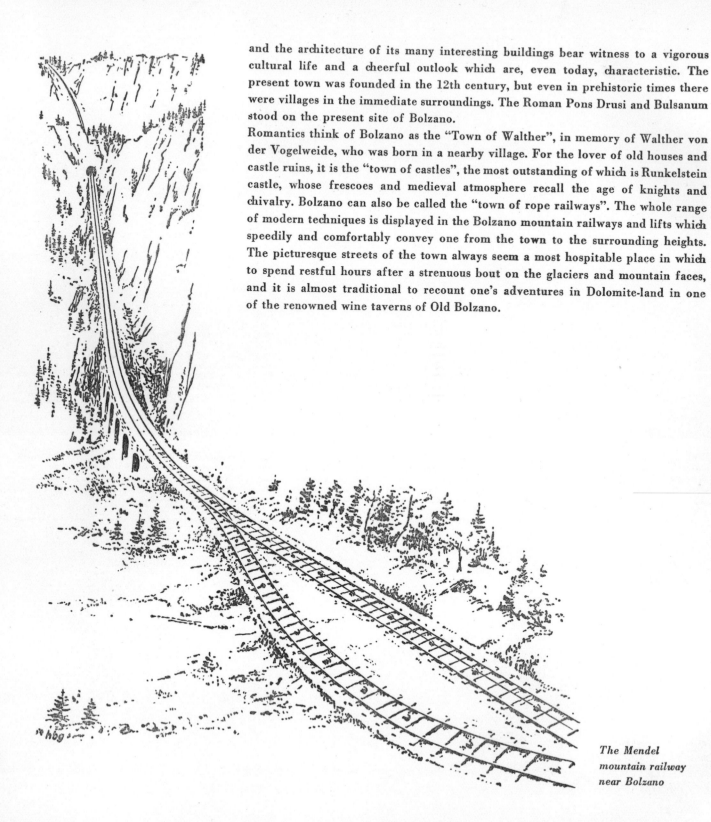

and the architecture of its many interesting buildings bear witness to a vigorous cultural life and a cheerful outlook which are, even today, characteristic. The present town was founded in the 12th century, but even in prehistoric times there were villages in the immediate surroundings. The Roman Pons Drusi and Bulsanum stood on the present site of Bolzano.

Romantics think of Bolzano as the "Town of Walther", in memory of Walther von der Vogelweide, who was born in a nearby village. For the lover of old houses and castle ruins, it is the "town of castles", the most outstanding of which is Runkelstein castle, whose frescoes and medieval atmosphere recall the age of knights and chivalry. Bolzano can also be called the "town of rope railways". The whole range of modern techniques is displayed in the Bolzano mountain railways and lifts which speedily and comfortably convey one from the town to the surrounding heights. The picturesque streets of the town always seem a most hospitable place in which to spend restful hours after a strenuous bout on the glaciers and mountain faces, and it is almost traditional to recount one's adventures in Dolomite-land in one of the renowned wine taverns of Old Bolzano.

*The Mendel*
*mountain railway*
*near Bolzano*